HowExpert Guide to Archery

101 Tips to Learn How to Shoot a Bow & Arrow, Improve Your Archery Skills, and Become a Better Archer

HowExpert with Miguel Rocha

Copyright HowExpert™
www.HowExpert.com

For more tips related to this topic, visit HowExpert.com/archery.

Recommended Resources

- HowExpert.com – Quick 'How To' Guides on All Topics from A to Z by Everyday Experts.
- HowExpert.com/free – Free HowExpert Email Newsletter.
- HowExpert.com/books – HowExpert Books
- HowExpert.com/courses – HowExpert Courses
- HowExpert.com/clothing – HowExpert Clothing
- HowExpert.com/membership – HowExpert Membership Site
- HowExpert.com/affiliates – HowExpert Affiliate Program
- HowExpert.com/jobs – HowExpert Jobs
- HowExpert.com/writers – Write About Your #1 Passion/Knowledge/Expertise & Become a HowExpert Author.
- HowExpert.com/resources – Additional HowExpert Recommended Resources
- YouTube.com/HowExpert – Subscribe to HowExpert YouTube.
- Instagram.com/HowExpert – Follow HowExpert on Instagram.
- Facebook.com/HowExpert – Follow HowExpert on Facebook.
- TikTok.com/@HowExpert – Follow HowExpert on TikTok.

Publisher's Foreword

Dear HowExpert Reader,

HowExpert publishes quick 'how to' guides on all topics from A to Z by everyday experts.

At HowExpert, our mission is to discover, empower, and maximize everyday people's talents to ultimately make a positive impact in the world for all topics from A to Z...one everyday expert at a time!

All of our HowExpert guides are written by everyday people just like you and me, who have a passion, knowledge, and expertise for a specific topic.

We take great pride in selecting everyday experts who have a passion, real-life experience in a topic, and excellent writing skills to teach you about the topic you are also passionate about and eager to learn.

We hope you get a lot of value from our HowExpert guides, and it can make a positive impact on your life in some way. All of our readers, including you, help us continue living our mission of positively impacting the world for all spheres of influences from A to Z.

If you enjoyed one of our HowExpert guides, then please take a moment to send us your feedback from wherever you got this book.

Thank you, and we wish you all the best in all aspects of life.

Sincerely,

BJ Min
Founder & Publisher of HowExpert
HowExpert.com

PS...If you are also interested in becoming a HowExpert author, then please visit our website at HowExpert.com/writers. Thank you & again, all the best!

Table of Contents

Introduction

Archery has been around for 10,000 years dating back to the stone age. It is perhaps the oldest and most refined weapon in history. Arguably it is the inspiration behind all modern weapons. The bow and arrow could be considered the great great great grandfather of today's rifles. With that being said, it has, however, withstood the test of time. When the rest of the world moved forward, archery stayed around. It has been adopted and transformed into a sport worldwide—a classic art that appears in movies and tv, earth's most elegant weapon. It is no wonder that the film industry has taken such a liking to the bow. Not only does it have a long, rich history, but it's also very marketable in films such as The Lord of the Rings, The Hunger Games, Arrow, and even the Avengers. All major forms of media found success around a protagonist with a bow. In all honesty, these same movies and TV shows inspired many arches to pick up their first bow. Any modern-day archer would be lying if they told you that they didn't get a little inspiration from their favorite bow-wielding superhero.

The oldest form of the bow was the longbow. Of course, as technology improved over the centuries, it was adapted into different shapes to suit the archer's needs. For example, Attila the Hun adopted a shorter version of the bow to be shot on horseback. The Japanese have a unique longbow where the bottom end of the bow is faster than the top. The archers of mid-evil England had bows up to 6 feet long. The versatility of the bow is unmatched, and even today, it continues to diversify. The modern archers of today have a variety of bows and tools at their disposal. Stabilizers, sights, arrow rests, quivers. Compounds and Recurves. The list goes on and on. This is not to mention the variety of arrows and broadheads. Each archer is encouraged to customize their bows to their liking. It is perhaps the most customizable weapon on the planet. One would be hard-pressed to find two completely identical bows, and archers find a sense of pride in that. Whatever way you decide to make your bow, know it is entirely your own and personalized to you alone.

Aside from the evolution and customization of the bow, there has been an evolution of the art itself. Nobody is waging war with arrows anymore; instead, it has become the primary weapon of many hunters. The primal nature of the bow has given hunters the impression that the bow is the fairest way to hunt their prey. The sport has also established itself as a respected event in the Olympics. In addition to the Olympics, competitions for both Recurve and Compound bows have become internationally widespread. Both forms of archery require vastly different bows and techniques but are essentially the same at their core. With that in mind, it's no easy feat to take up archery. You must find out several things about yourself to shoot a bow. Things such as draw length, how much weight you can pull back, even something like your vision must be tested to customize the bow to your liking. While all of this is not necessarily required for a starter bow and archer, you will need them to create a bow to your measurements and shoot at high efficiency.

It is important to remember that archery is not a fast-paced salsa but rather a slow ballet. It will take a year to get good and many more to master. Strengthening your mind and body is just as important as proper form and technique. You will find that the sport is a much more taxing sport than it appears. Shooting two dozen arrows will exhaust your muscles just as much as weight training. Within the context of this book, you will receive a plethora of tips for beginner and intermediate level archers, as well as some helpful illustrations for specific techniques. Not only will you pick up tips for your form, but as well as conditioning tips for your body.

Lesson 1: The Equipment

The 10 Essentials for a Starter Archer

<u>Tip 1: Know your bow.</u>

It is understood that one should know everything about the equipment that they are using. Ignorance is the enemy of progress, and in the case of archery, everyone needs instructions at first. There are four distinct types of bows: Longbow, Recurve, Compound, and Crossbows. We will not be going over how the crossbow because the techniques are more reminiscent of a firearm than a bow, and most archery tools do not apply to the crossbow. The Longbow and Recurve are built differently but house identical techniques. We will break the bow into two categories, compounds, and longbows/recurves, for the sake of categorization.

It is essential to know the distinction between these two categories because an expert in one is not always an expert in the other. This is not to say that the techniques are vastly different because they are not; it is the feel of the different bows that often throw off new archers. You will find the longbow to be much more challenging to shoot, but the compound is the more powerful of the two. Deciding between the two bows is a matter of preference. Typically, hunters favor the compound for its power and compatibility. On the other hand, longbows and recurves are used more commonly for competitions such as the Olympics.

Tip 2: Know the difference between a recurve and a compound!

Traditional Bows:

There are advantages and disadvantages to each bow. One advantage to the traditional style of bows is their survivability. Unlike the complicated mechanics of the compound, traditional bows have much fewer parts to maintain. Survival experts prefer them over compound bows because of their easy-to-maintain nature. With a flexible enough branch and some rope, any handy archer can make a longbow. Of course, that is not the most significant thing the traditional bow has over the compound. The most important advantage the traditional bow holds is its prominence in archery. While compounds are allowed in elite competitions against other compounds, the conventional bow stands the larger of the two titans.

Traditional bows have remained the only category of archery in the Olympics since introduced to the games. It is the original form of archery. The form and strength required to shoot the traditional bows place a significant burden on the archers in this craft because the skill gap between archers is much more apparent. You can see why that is an essential factor in terms of competition. If an archer had no interest in hunting and only sought to improve for sport, then the traditional bow would be the path to take. There has been a push to include compounds into the games, but it is an uphill battle, so it seems that traditional bows may maintain their death grips in the world of archery.

Choosing the traditional bow over the compound bow does not come without some disadvantages. If I have not made it clear enough, the classic bow is much more challenging to shoot. Even with the help of every tool in the sport, the traditional bow is trumped by the compound in terms of user-friendliness and effectiveness. With this bow, you have to worry about aiming and hold the draw at your anchor, finger release, keeping the bow leveled, the list goes on. It takes a lot of effort to master this craft, and even if you did, your range in comparison to the compound would be much shorter. A 100-yard shot may prove challenging for any recurve archer, but the task would be easy for a competent archer with a compound.

Compound Bow:

Compounds are the future bows but are scarce in most countries. It is a western dominated weapon and is only really used for hunting. With good reason, too, the compound bow is made to be easy and effective. Despite having a higher draw weight, the bow is much easier to hold at your anchor point. This is due to the pulley system that the bow is built with, or the "cam." Unlike the traditional bow, the tension that launches the arrows does not come from the bending of the bow's arms but the tension from the cam. With this system, when an archer draws their bow and reaches their anchor point, the draw weight significantly decreases. This eases many burdens with the archer. Coupled with the various tools to help aim and stabilize and extensive range, shooting is straightforward. Most youth bows sold are low draw weight compound bows. The easy nature of the bow makes it a good starter bow for beginners; a youth bow can hunt small game if desired. Of course, an adult bow is more favorable in any hunting situation.

When it comes to hunting, the compound dominantly controls the sport. While it recurves and longbows are used for hunting, the shorter range and greater difficulty make it a less favorable choice. Compounds, despite their various components, are easier to store. The cam system does not place any significant tension on any parts of the bow, unlike the arms of a traditional bow. If someone looked to store the bow for extended periods, they would simply need to place it in a case until it was called upon again. With a recurve, it would be best to take it apart for storage to preserve the tension of the bow arms.

With all this said, the compound is not perfect. It is significantly more expensive than the traditional bow. A decent conventional bow can be found for 200 dollars, and for beginners, there are good bows for as low as 100. The compound, however, averages upwards of 400 dollars. Sometimes without any of the necessary bow tools, arrow rests, sights, and stabilizers, quivers, etc. An expensive hobby if you are not a hunter, and if you aspire to be an Olympian, you will not get there with a compound.

The cam system was created in 1966 with the invention of the first compound bow. Its ability to be fine-tuned to the user and its high power has made it the favorite of hunters.

Tip 3: Be able to shoot both.

This is not so much a tip but a strong recommendation. The ability to shoot both types of bows is what separates the good archers from the experts. As previously stated, one expert in one is not always an expert on the other. The sport of archery is not so one-dimensional that you should only stick to one form of the bow. It is both fun and imperative that you learn to shoot both to refine your fundamentals. The feel of each bow may be different, but the techniques to shoot them are the same. When learning both bows, consider which bow feels the most natural to you. Some favor the ease of the compound, while others like the look of the traditional.

Tip 4: Get the proper equipment.

If you think that the bow itself is all you need, then your wallet is in for a rude awakening. To shoot at your absolute best, you must equip yourself with all the right tools to set you up for success. This is where the image of the bow in media is contorted into a less appealing form. In movies and tv shows, the bow is typically stripped of its extra parts to maintain a sleeker appearance. While there is nothing wrong with shooting a naked bow, it can prove more complicated than it seems. Shooting a barebow is a lot of instinct and good intuition, but now, with technology's help, that factor has been removed.

Tip 5: Find the perfect sights.

The most expensive attachment of the bow, the sights, is also the most important for a modern-day archer, and typically your local sporting goods store can zero it in for you. It consists of two main components: the level and the sight pins. First, it comes with a small level in your line of sight to indicate if you are not shooting the bow tilted. This is important because the aerodynamics of the arrow is most effective when fired from a leveled bow. The second component, the sight pins, are used to shoot at different ranges. Unlike the scope of a rifle, the sights of a bow have multiple. "Crosshairs." The top pin is used for shorter distances, while the lower pins are used for farther distances. Some sights will come with three pins, and others can have up to five. The more pins, the easier it is to shoot at various ranges.

(A standard sight typically comes with three sight pins and a level indicator)

Tip 6: Use a proper arrow rest.

An arrow rest's primary purpose is safety. While all bows have an arrow shelf, the indentation in the bow is the most primitive form of arrow rest. Archers who attempt to shoot with just the arrow shelf will find it challenging to keep the arrow in place. The arrow will often slide off the shelf and the bow with new archers. This can be extremely dangerous for yourself and anyone around you. If someone were to misfire with the arrow hanging off the rest, it could result in severe bodily injury to the archer's limbs or anyone around them.

In most cases, a simple plastic rest will suffice, but there is a variety of arrow rests on choosing from for the more severe archers. The whisker biscuit is the most typical rest, but it can slightly reduce the arrow's speed. Hunters prefer more mechanical rests that minimize the friction of the arrow.

This is the most common arrow rest, nicknamed the "Whisker Biscuit." It's simple and user-friendly. Unfortunately, it does slightly slow down the arrow. Professional archers favor more complex and expensive arrow rests.

Tip 7: Use a stabilizer!

The stabilizer is just a fancy term for a heavy metal rod. It increases the weight of the bow to increase stability and decrease movement on the release. In addition, it helps reduce the inconsistencies of the archer's release by adding to the moment of inertia of the bow. If you watch professional archers shooting at competitions, you will notice strange metal rods sticking out of the front of their bow; those are stabilizers. Stabilizers can vary from small rods to crazy tripods. For new archers, I would suggest a simple, inexpensive one.

Tip 8: Use a release.

The release is one of the trickiest parts about shooting a bow. Traditionally archers use three fingers to hold the string, but the problem with that method is it can cause vibrations in the string during launch. It is exceedingly difficult to have a seamless release shooting with just your fingers. It can also cause unnecessary tension in the archer's form. When this happens, the archer may flinch upon release and throw the arrow off trajectory. A mechanical release removes the friction that would be created from your fingers to ensure a seamless release every time. This will make your shots much more consistent, thus improving your accuracy.

Even amongst competition archers, some form of the release is used. Olympic archers, however, are not permitted such equipment.

Tip 9: Do not cheap out on arrows.

Archery is an expensive sport, and I would be lying to you if I said it was not. Everything from the bow to the parts of the bow adds up to quite the dent in your wallet. Unfortunately, Arrows are no exception. You would think that the most expendable part of archery would be the cheapest; it is not. A pack of decent arrows is upwards of 30 dollars US (United States). A costly purchase considering how often you will lose them. However, it is worth the expense because each bow requires specific arrows. If you were to try and shoot an arrow uncut, then you will find your shots to be far off it is intended mark. The nature of the bow is that it can only shoot what it can handle. Just like bullet calibers for a firearm, bows need specific arrow spines. If you were to buy a dozen 4-dollar wooden arrows from your local Walmart, then yes, you would have saved some money at the cost of never hitting a bullseye ever again. Simply put, do not cheap out on arrows.

Tip 10: Replace your Equipment!

Bows may seem like they last forever, but they do not. You should replace the parts of your bow often, bowstrings in particular. When your bowstring starts to fray, it is best to get it replaced as soon as possible to prevent any unfortunate destruction of your bow. For recurve bows, replace the arms when you notice cracking or chipping. A well-maintained bow can last upwards of 30 years, but you must put in the effort to make it last. Do not shoot till it explodes in your face and act surprised when it does.

Chapter Review

The most significant takeaway point from this lesson is that knowledge is half the battle. An inexperienced archer can take a bow and shoot it at a broadside of a barn, but it is the knowledge of the equipment that will make it accurate. Just like any sport, you must know the equipment that you are using. Archers must be diverse and well-informed about the equipment that they use. It would be difficult for anyone to dig a hole with a spoon but give them a shovel, and things become much more manageable. This same concept applies to archery. Keep your equipment well maintained, and choose the tools carefully. The different parts of a bow are various tools, each with a specific purpose, and you must know what that purpose is.

Lesson 2: Shooting

The 10 Essentials to Good Shooting Form

Tip 11: Control your breathing.

Like any other sharpshooter sport, the key to aiming lies in your breathing. Shooting mid-breath will create an inconsistency in the altitude of your shot. Shooting during an inhale will make your shot rise, while shooting during an exhale will make it fall. When any expert shooter aims in his/her designated sport, they hold their breath like they are too focused on their target they can do nothing else. This is natural for anyone trying to aim a bow or rifle. However, there is a small trick that does not always come naturally to people. Instead of breathing in and holding your breath, breathe out and shoot at that pause after your breath. That small window is when your body is most relaxed and still.

The trouble with shooting with air still in your lungs creates tension in your chest that will make it difficult to relax, and relaxing is the most important part of shooting. Your lungs are not meant to house an excess of air for extended periods. Biologically they process the air and exhale it in a matter of seconds, so it feels unnatural when they are stored in your lungs for extended periods. Try it, breath a large amount of air in and hold it, then try and breath out and hold it. You will find that your lungs are more comfortable being empty rather than full. Comfortability is paramount to keeping still when shooting in any form of marksmanship.

Tip 12: Correct your stance.

When teaching new archers how to shoot, I find that the most common thing they all do is stand almost square with the target, like they are trying to stand behind the arrow to aim it. This is very wrong. The proper stance in archery is to stand parallel with the target with feet shoulder with apart. The bow is an extension of your arm and chest and must be aimed as such. With your arm fully extended, pointing at the target, you must bring the string all the way to your chest. It will seem uncomfortably close initially, but as it becomes more natural, you will see what I mean when I say that the bow is an extension of your body.

As for aiming, you will be bringing the arrow as close to your face and lips as possible. This is called the anchor point. The anchor point is the point that you are aiming at full draw. Typically, the anchor point will be at the corner of your mouth. That is where the bend of the string will sit. Sometimes, archers will bring the anchor point a little higher to their cheek to get their eye closer to the arrow's shaft, thus making it easier to aim.

Tip 13: Let the strings slip off your finger.

The release is the trickiest part about archery. Fortunately, this is often countered with a mechanical release. When a mechanical release is not an option (In competitions), then it is important that you learn to "finger shoot." Finger shooting is when you are holding the string with your fingers like a traditional archer. A skill often lost to today's modern archers and their mechanical release. You see, a mechanical release is like a trigger mechanism for bows. It removes all jerking or fumbles during the launch of the arrow, ensuring a clean shot. A great invention for hunters and recreational archers, but those with eyes set on the competitive scene, the release will be forty percent of your skillset. I cannot stress this enough; you want a completely seamless transition during launch. If any vibration or jerking is added to the arrow during take-off, it may result in a missed shot. The best way to do this is to let the arrow slip of your fingers. Do not try to suddenly release your fingers from the string or yank them off. I assure you; it will not be a pretty shot. It may hurt new archers but letting the fingers slowly slip off your fingers is the best way to maintain a consistent shot grouping. I also suggest a small finger guard if desired. It will also make the slip of the sting smoother opposed to the rough texture of calloused hands.

Tip 14: Open both eyes

This is a stranger tip, considering anyone that has ever aimed anything typically closes one eye to focus on their target as they should, but being able to shoot with both eyes open allows for a larger field of vision. You will be able to take in more data, such as wind patterns or movements that may affect your shot. This is more imperative to hunters than target archers. Hunters, you may want to aim with both eyes open. It will make you a keener hunter and deadlier archer. It is simply a helpful tool to improve your feel for the bow and target acquisition in terms of target shooting.

Tip 15: Do not try and shoot too fast.

A misconception about archers is that the more skilled an archer is, the faster they can shoot. While it does take considerable skill to shoot a volley of arrows in a short amount of time, it is highly impractical. There will never be a realistic situation for an archer to have to shoot as fast as Hawkeye from the Avengers. The ability to shoot fast is more of a party trick than a practical skill. It may be cool to shoot at the speed of a superhero for a zombie apocalypse, but in all reality, a hunter only gets one shot, and an Olympian only must shoot three arrows at a time.

In an archery tournament, an archer is given 2 minutes to shoot three arrows or, in some cases, 4 minutes to shoot six arrows. As for hunters, they only get one shot. If a hunter misses, their prey will get spooked and run away. In both these cases, speed is not a factor. To maximize your accuracy as an archer, you must learn to relax and shoot at your own pace. It will not benefit you in any situation to empty your quiver so quickly. This also applies to practice. Do not practice shooting fast. Instead, practice aiming and holding the arrow at your anchor. Archery is a slow dance, not a salsa.

Tip 16: Aim small, miss small.

In the beginning, it may seem frustrating to not be able to hit a bullseye, and you may find yourself content with simply hitting the target. While it is important to not be so hard on yourself, it is also important to hold yourself to a standard. Those satisfied with just hitting the target tend to aim for the target instead of focusing on the bullseye. When you lower your standards, your skill ceiling will lower as well. Aim for the smallest point on your target every single time, and you will find your arrows are grouped much tighter together. If this is the case, and they are still off your mark, then it may be an issue of zeroing in your sights rather than human error. If you maintain your standard for excellence and hold yourself accountable for mistakes or bad form, your aim will continue to improve exponentially.

Tip 17: Shoot standing straight up.

Proper archery form is when an archer is standing up straight and tall with the bow leveled to the ground.

Your body should be in the shape of a T. Often, in television and other forms of media, archers are portrayed shooting the bow angled, with the archer slightly hunched over. This form is reminiscent of medieval archers. A handful of archers shoot with this form, although most do always shoot traditional bows. If someone were to attempt to shoot a compound bow with this form, it would prove difficult and potentially dangerous. It is best to use proper form when learning and practicing removing any unnecessary complications. With that being said, a lot of the fun in archery is pushing your skills to the limit. Learning the medieval form could prove to be a pleasant change of pace further down the line. Until you have mastered shooting basics, do not stray from the form taught to all beginner archers.

Tip 18: Three fingers on the string

Three fingers on the string are the proper way to draw the string back. A misconception is that archers only pull back with two fingers, one on top and one on the bottom. Not only is this wrong, but it is exceedingly difficult and sometimes painful. The pointer, middle, and ring will allow the most grip strength without sacrificing a seamless release. If you attempt to shoot with your pinky on the string as well, you will find it difficult to let the string slip off your fingers without getting caught on it. The traditional way to go about it is one finger on top, two on the button. Some archers like to put three fingers on the bottom so that they may bring the arrow closer to their line of sight; this is most helpful when shooting a recurve or longbow rather than a compound.

Tip 19: Do not be afraid to shoot long range.

Shooting great distances may seem extremely difficult, but it is easier than you may think. With the proper arrow rest, sights, and stabilizer, any bow can hit long distances with ease. Even with a naked bow, attempting to shoot long distances is good practice. If someone misses by a foot at 15 yards, they may completely miss the target at 50. Shooting at long-distance removes any acceptable margin of error, thus forcing you to get everything right. Your breathing, release, and grip are all considered when shooting at greater distances. Challenging yourself is the only way to improve, and finding success in those difficult obstacles will grant you a new level of confidence.

To accurately assess your accuracy, you should be shooting arrows right on top of each other at 15 yards, and as you get further back, the groupings may spread out gradually. At 50+, your groupings should not be more than 18 inches from each other. It is quite all right if they are, but it is a sign that there is room for improvement. Practice shooting at 50 yards often, and do not be afraid to attempt 100 when you are comfortable with your level of accuracy. If you find yourself comfortably shooting at great distances, you have truly become an expert in the sport.

Tip 20: Practice often

Any skill requires practice to become perfect. Archey is no different and the biggest advocate of the saying. Aside from recreational archers, it is a high-stakes sport. If a hunter is not skilled in his craft, they may end up causing a great deal of pain to their prey. As a hunter, the humane and swift execution of your prey should be a top priority. Despite widespread belief, hunters are very in tuned with nature and have profound respect for the animals and forest. Even those with no intentions to hunt must understand that archery can be dangerous, and practicing safe habits is an essential part of that sport. Practice often, and your understanding of the bow, as well as your skills, will continue to improve. Joining a local archery club will provide you with an accessible bow and local trainers to help you fine-tune your form.

Chapter Review

This lesson is all about the fundamentals of archery and shooting with proper form. At its core, archery is a sport of marksmanship. Accuracy is the number one priority, and an archer must maximize that. Minor adjustments like controlling your breathing, correcting your stance, and choosing where you aim can make drastic changes in the accuracy of your shot. Often you will see untrained archers shooting with very questionable form. If not addressed early, it can create bad habits that will be difficult to break. The key to an expert archer is a solid foundation. It is important to remember the fundamentals and build on them as you progress through your archery journey with this lesson.

Lesson 3: Making Practice Fun and Effective

The 10 Essentials to Practicing Efficiently.

<u>*Tip 21: Start young*</u>

A benefit I had growing up is that I began archery lessons when I was 13. As I grew up, I upgraded bows and began to shoot farther and more consistently. It was nice. As I aged, my skills naturally developed, and by the time I was 18, I was shooting at Olympic qualifiers. Even now, with archery as just a hobby and extended periods between practices, it comes naturally to me. My accuracy suffers minimal depreciation with time, credited to the skills instilled in me when I was incredibly young.

Starting young may not be an option for everyone, but it is not the youth that makes archery a natural skill; it is the years of dedication. Be patient and know that as time passes, your routines will become second nature. Shooting may require a lot of focusing within the first year, but you will draw your bow, aim, and fire during your fifth, without hesitation.

<u>*Tip 22: Warm-up at the short-range*</u>

For those who have not been shooting for multiple years, and even those who have, there is no shame in shooting at short range. Warming up is a practice for all sports. Shooting at short ranges helps dial in your form and routine so that when it comes to shooting at longer, more difficult targets, you will be mentally and physically prepared. Even the most expert archers will forget a step or two of their routine as they warm up. Shooting at short ranges and holding yourself to a perfect standard at those ranges will make shooting at longer ranges feel more doable. If you were to dive into the longer ranges right from the get-go, then you are going to lose a couple of arrows as you warm up.

Tip 23: Shoot at different ranges

Do not grow too comfortable with one singular range. I am guilty of this. For many years I was content with only shooting at 20 yards, but in the end, it deterred my growth. It is easy to find a comfortable range and stay there; your shots are consistent, and your confidence grows with each shot. Unfortunately, that does not improve your overall skill as an archer. To improve in any sport, you must challenge yourself during those uncomfortable moments. Basketball players can use their off-hand, baseball players can play any position if needed, and archers are not limited in range. Shoot at the 50, take a couple of shots at 100 unload your quiver at the 20. Do not be afraid to mix it up. Being able to judge your distance and adjust to the change in trajectory will ensure you are ready for any situation as an archer.

Tip 24: Get your own targets.

This is more of a friendly reminder, bring some extra targets to the range! Most ranges will already have targets on, but typically they are very worn out. It will be hard to mark your hits or sometimes even see your targets with the number of arrows that have passed through the targets. A simple bullseye target will serve its purpose. Bring a few extra copies if you intend to test the sights on your bow. It will save you the pain of trying to find viable targets to shoot at and competing for a good lane at the range. New targets are essential for the next tip.

Tip 25: Write it down.

Write down your results. Tracking your progress will show you how far you have come and helped set new realistic goals for the future. Bring a small journal and record how far you shot and how well your groupings were. Here you can write down some of the essential tips you found helpful or a checklist of your routine. Record keeping may seem like a trivial task, but you will appreciate yourself when you can look back and see the progress you have made. It will be a helpful tool that you go back to as you continue your path as an archer.

Tip 26: Make it a pasttime.

Practice can seem tedious at times, and when it becomes so, archery may start to bore you. When boredom begins to set in, your techniques become lazy. Do not let yourself get to this point. Do practice a pastime and enjoy yourself. You do not have to be confined to one archery lane, repetitively shooting six arrows downrange. Try different techniques to keep it interesting, socialize with other archers, bring some food. In my years of archery, I have met many archers, and the best ones never took practice too seriously. The older archers are always sitting around laughing and socializing between heats. Practice is a social event for them, and that is why archery has never gotten boring for them after decades of archery. Continue to love the sport and continue to have fun with it, and with time and practice, it will come naturally to you.

Tip 27: Take breaks

Archery may seem to be a tireless sport, but you will feel fatigued after launching a couple of dozen arrows downrange. Many people seem to think that you can shoot a hundred arrows without compromising your form to fatigue. This is false. Even a low draw weight bow can fatigue your muscles if put through enough repetitions. A compound bow, for example, is on average 60 pounds. After two heats at the range, you would have pulled 60 pounds 12 times in a matter of a few minutes. Imagine doing that a hundred times. You will feel fatigued, and when you do, your form will begin to falter. Do not be afraid to take a break after a few iterations of arrows. It will prolong your endurance and ensure more consistent practice.

Tip 28: Find a good archery range.

By archery range, I mean an official range. You can only get so far by practicing in your backyard. Unless you have multiple acres of land, then it is that you do not have the space to shoot at a proper distance for practicing archery. Archery ranges are more common than you may think. A simple google search may do the trick. Your local Bass Pro Shop typically allows free use of their range as well. Make sure your range has adequate space in both length and width. Ensure there is a proper hill or wall at the end of the range, so the arrow stops and does not continue onward to injure someone or damage anything. There should be a list of range rules posted somewhere visible, as well as a range supervisor. For the safety of everyone at the range, everyone must abide by the same rules and range etiquette. The most important rule is that everyone ceases fire at the same time so that nobody is downrange during a volley of arrows being fired.

Tip 29: Shoot indoors if you can.

Most archery ranges are outdoors, which allows for more space to shoot. However, some rare cases in an indoor range can provide adequate space to shoot longer distances. When this becomes available, be sure to seize the opportunity. Indoor ranges eliminate any extra factors in your shot/form, such as wind, humidity, and sunlight. Your arrow lands where you aim in the indoor range, making it much easier to fine-tune your skills. If your sight and bow are tuned, anything less than a bull's eye is human error. You should consider any flaws you make when shooting and correct them indoors before proceeding to an outdoor range. Consider the indoor range a controlled test area for your bow.

Tip 30: Develop a routine

Routines are repetitive behaviors, and when you find a routine that helps you aim dead center, you found a good routine. Practice doing the same thing every time and make a mental checklist of the things you do before each shot, such as how you put your arrow on its rest, the way you breathe, checking the level, and aiming with the same sight pin. Everything can be a factor in shooting your bow, so you must make sure that you have done everything in your power to shoot straight. The routine simply helps keep yourself in check. If you miss your target, it may have been because you did not check the level of your bow, or you put your arrow on crooked, which are all things that can be prevented by developing a routine.

Chapter Review

Practice can be tedious with any sport. More often than not, it's a long and boring use of your time. With archery, it does not need to be this way. With lesson 3, archers will learn to maximize their practice and make it a pastime rather than a formal exercise. The essential tips in this lesson require patience. An archer does not have to run through a hundred arrows in an hour for training to be effective. Instead, archers must pace themselves. Take breaks, write down your results and warm up before any serious target shooting. Routines will be an archer's best friend when they are practicing. The proper form practiced in routines will carry over to the more serious competitions or hunting seasons. If you practice the right way, you will develop into a fine archer with excellent skills and an understanding of your bow.

Lesson 4: Building Your Range

The 10 Essentials to Creating Your Own Space to Shoot.

Tip 31: Use lots of open space

For some, going to a range is not always an option. The convenience of having your range at home lets you practice more often without sacrificing any time of your day. Although not set up correctly, an at-home range can be dangerous and sometimes counterproductive to your training. The first and the most important thing needed for an at-home range is space. I would not suggest converting your backyard into a range if you live in the suburbs. A misfire or wild ricochet could result in severe injury or property damage. If you are fortunate enough to own or live on multiple acres of land, then an at-home range is much more realistic for you. Keep in mind that typically 15 yards is the closest target at most ranges, but most practice at the 20-yard target. Even so, I would highly recommend at least 30 yards of room at the bare minimum. This assumes you are still new to the sport and have no desire to attempt long-distance shots yet. If you are not new to the sport, I recommend 100 yards of room to play with. In either case, you want to be away from any neighbors or neighborhoods.

Tip 32: Shoot with a hill

Shooting on flat land is perfectly fine, but keep in mind that you may lose a couple of arrows during your practice. A hill at the back of your range can prevent this problem and prevent any wild arrows from flying off to the distance to hurt or damage something. The key to any range is to establish a limit for projectiles. At gun ranges, they have walls or large hills to stop bullets. Archery ranges are no exception. The chances of a projectile flying off to the distance and damaging something are slim but never zero. Shooting with a hill to stop arrows is a good safety measure to take when creating your range. Even a mound of dirt will stop an arrow in its tracks and save you the trouble of looking for an arrow in an open field.

Tip 33: Shoot at an elevation

The fun part about having your range is that you can customize it to your liking. Hunters, more specifically, will typically be shooting from a tree stand at a higher elevation than their target. A tree stand helps hunters see at a greater distance while also leaving a smaller footprint on the environment. The list goes on, but it is widely accepted as the best technique for archers. With this, it is crucial to practice your craft in the most realistic ways. Shooting at a higher elevation downhill towards a target may be the best way to replicate a tree stand shot outside of an actual tree stand. The luxury of a tree stand is not always offered at every range, so you should take advantage of the situation and attempt to mimic one when creating your own. This is not only for hunters but target archers as well. Shooting at an elevation can increase your range and help you hit targets typically too far for you.

Tip 34: Shoot with the wind at your back

Nobody can control the wind, but we can read the direction it comes from. There are parts of the world that have prevailing winds. This is a type of wind that only blows in one direction. I realize that it is rare and unrealistic to ask for, but if you find yourself in that type of area, take advantage of it. As for the rest of us, the benefit of having our own space is that we are not limited to shooting in only one direction. That is why it is vital to find an area that is long and wide. Take the time to make it easier on yourself and adjust your targets to be downwind. The wind at your back will help with your range and eliminate any drifting from your arrows. While I encourage archers to challenge themselves, it is also essential to set yourself up for success.

Tip 35: Know your range.

In hunting, you will not be able to determine how far away your target is. In target archery, you will fire at the same distance every time. In both situations, you must be able to accurately judge and recognize the distance of the target. When setting up your range, knowing exactly how far away you are shooting will help you aim correctly and teach you to recognize what certain distances look like. While shooting at odd ranges does help you improve as an archer, it is ineffective training when you begin to think twenty yards is thirty or vice versa. A good rule of thumb is one pace equals one yard. This rule will help for shorter distances, but I would recommend a rangefinder for the longer distance. Once you begin to understand what twenty yards look like, then you will be able to shoot more accurately at any distance.

Tip 36: Switch ranges between shots

The fun part about having your range is that you do not have to worry about range courtesy, so have fun with it. Shoot at multiple targets, all at different ranges. This drill will help you think faster and improve your reaction time. Typically, in a formal archery range, you are confined to one lane at one distance. You are not limited to that with your range. Buy multiple targets and set them up in a way that you can shoot at them from a stationary position. Not only is this a fun drill that will make practicing fun, but it is also an amazingly effective drill that helps you recognize the different ranges and how to adjust to them.

Tip 37: Shoot at different targets

Any type of target will serve its purpose. There is no
such thing as one target being better than another.
However, each target can require a different level of
focus. Some targets are prominent and highly visible,
some are smaller, and some are plastic animals.
Having a variety of targets will force you to adjust
your aim with each variation. Large targets are
excellent from a general target archery standpoint,
while smaller targets require more focus and accuracy
to hit. Hunters, I suggest occasionally using a foam
animal on occasion. Hunting requires precise hits for
a humane elimination. A shot to the leg or hind of an
animal will not suffice. It is essential to practice
avoiding these with a life-like target.

_Most ranges will come with a variety of paper
targets. Some will even include 3D targets for
hunters._

Tip 38: Be practical

Practicality is key to good practicing. What I mean by this is to shoot with a proper bow and proper targets. Do not attempt to shoot huge arching shots for longer distances or shoot your bow angled like Robin Hood. There are several videos up on YouTube that try to teach archers how to curve their arrows, shoot with their feet, etc.; anything to add flare to the sport. You will find videos of other archers speculating how ancient archers use to fire their bows exceptionally fast or shoot kneeling. These videos tend to romanticize the notion of ancient archery. Everyone wishes that the archers like Legolas from the Lord of the Rings existed; the world of archery would be much more exciting if that level of skill were achievable. Unfortunately, the matter is that archery in today's modern age is just not that exciting. Target archers shoot stationary in one lane while hunters sit in treetops firing a singular arrow per hunt. So do not attempt to build an outrageous range or use an ancient longbow. Be practical with your range and live in the 21st century. This, of course, is not to knock on any historians that wish to study the ancient archers because it is an admirable passion and study, but not for anyone trying to hunt or enter in a competition.

Tip 39: Be realistic

Practicality and realism go hand in hand. The freedom to have your range is that you do not necessarily need to be realistic—a fun notion and a dangerous one. While I am sure there is some archer out there skilled enough and confident enough to shoot an apple atop a friend's head, I would not recommend it being a means of practice. If you are fortunate enough to own enough land for an archery range and fortunate enough to own a horse, do not attempt to mix the two sports. It will not go well. In terms of modern archery, you must be realistic with your range and practice. I encourage new archers to have fun with it and to try different techniques, but to stay within the parameters of realistic archery.

Tip 40: Crank up the music.

Lastly, archery is meant to be fun! With your own space to shoot, you can truly make it into a pastime. Bring out food and crank up the music. Have fun while you are there, and practice will go by a lot faster. When you have fun with something, time will fly by a lot faster. You may not realize by the time you are done that you have been practicing for a couple of hours. This tricks you into getting in more repetitions. The more repetitions you run through, the more ingrained your routine will be.

Chapter Review

Some people don't have the luxury of a local archery club to practice at. In this case, making your archery range could be an option if you have space for it. The benefit of having your range is that it allows you to practice and shoot at your own pace. This does not mean that you should be shooting your bow in the backyard of your suburban neighborhood. Archery requires a lot of room for proper practice, and it would be dangerous to practice in a highly-populated area. The biggest thing to take away from this lesson is that your range must replicate a real archery range. Be practical, be realistic, and, most importantly, be safe. You can cut loose with your range and make it a pass time, but safety is always a priority.

Lesson 5: Building a Bow

The 10 Essentials to Building Your Own Archery Set Up.

Tip 41: Invest in your bow.

In chapter one, I emphasized the importance of your equipment. Now it is time to put it all together. If you truly want a good bow with good results, you have to drop a significant amount of money. A well-maintained bow will last you decades if taken care of properly. Think of the purchase as an investment. In most cases, you will only buy one or two bows in your lifetime unless you are a pro that fires an outrageous number of arrows. In that case, your bow may not last you as long. However, for most archers who shoot recreationally, buying a new bow will be a rare occasion. With that being said, invest in your bow. Put some serious thought into the equipment you purchase and don't cheap out on the important stuff.

The bow itself is, of course, the most important piece of equipment, and if you start young, you may outgrow your first bow. When it comes time to invest in your "forever bow," do the research and find the brand and model that suits you the best. I won't tell you what bow to get because everyone may have a different preference. Even minor details like the color of your bow are important. It is going to be with you for a long time, after all. Do not rush in purchasing one for the sake of having one. Wait till you find the perfect one for you.

When you do get that perfect bow, it will be time to decorate it with only the best parts. I went over each part in chapter one and the importance of each one. Refer back to chapter one, tip 4-9, for more details. It is unlikely that any bow part will break, so expect the equipment you buy for your bow to be more or less the bow's permanent parts. When choosing your sights, arrow rest, etc., know that there are levels to the quality of them. The differences between a cheap sight and expensive sight are much more noticeable than a cheap bow and an expensive bow. The equipment you choose is what makes the bow, so invest in them. You only get out of it what you put into it.

Tip 42: Make sure you are using the proper draw length.

A misunderstanding with the bow is that anyone can pick up any bow and shoot it. With traditional style bows, most people can pick it up and shoot it. This is not the case with compound bows. Compound bows come in different sizes, with varying weights of draw lengths. The draw length is how far you can pull the string back, and it has to be adjusted to each archer. Someone who is five foot eight will most likely have a shorter draw length than six foot two. If your draw length is too short or too long, you will not aim the bow correctly. Compound bows are so easy to aim due to the weight shifting down thanks to the cam. It allows you to hold the string for a longer time at your natural anchor point. If the bow doesn't allow you to pull it back to your anchor point or makes you pull past your anchor point, then you end up straining yourself, defeating the whole purpose of the cam system. Your draw length is the length of your arms from fingertip to fingertip, minus fifteen and divided by two.

Tip 43: Use a draw weight you can handle.

Bows are deceptively hard to pull back. On average most bows have a draw weight of 60 pounds, and that is considered fairly light for an archer. Some hunting bows reach up to 100 pounds, and some only have a draw weight of 40. Everybody has a different preference when it comes to the weight of their bow. Target bows typically favor lighter weights, while hunting bows prefer heavier weights. In either case, it is important for you to use a draw weight that you can handle. If you can't even pull back your bow, then you won't be able to fire it. I've seen many people misfire an arrow because their arms would fail before reaching their anchor point.

Tip 44: Learn your natural anchor.

It is fairly easy to find your anchor with a proper draw length. With a compound bow, and releases it is a no-brainer. Unfortunately, not all bows are gifted with a cam system, and there will be an occasion where you forget your release at home. If you have to finger shoot, you should know your anchor point without the release. Perhaps take it a step further and learn your anchor point on a traditional bow. It is an entirely different feeling shooting with your fingers on the string rather than using a release. The anchor point may shift slightly from your release anchor point and your natural anchor point. Typically, your anchor point is at the corner of your lip, but depending on the release, your fingers may be by your ear. There may be a disconnect between where your fingers typically are and where the string ends when transitioning to a natural anchor point. A good training tip is to shoot without the aid of a release first. Learning how to shoot without a release will make your life a lot easier when you start to use it.

The anchor point may shift up or down depending on your technique, but it should always stay at your draw length.

Tip 45: Use the proper arrow spine.

An arrow's spine rating is essentially how stiff the arrow is. When an arrow is launched at high speeds, it will bend in the air. There is a lot of physics involved, but in layman's terms, the different amount of force applied to the arrow as well as its length determines how much the arrow bends during flight. Bending during flight creates erratic flight patterns and inconsistent shot patterns. It is not enough to get the stiffest spine possible because a stiff spine with low weight will also cause some irregularities. The easiest answer for this is to consult with your local archery shop to determine what spine is best for your bow.

Tip 46: Get your arrows cut to length.

Arrows all come in the same length from the package, but they are meant to be cut. Unless you are a very tall archer with a long draw length, you will most likely need your arrows cut to your size. Much like the arrow spine, the length of the arrow and how it reacts to the force applied to it determines its flight path. If the arrow is too long for the bow, it will warp during flight because it is off balance. In every archery shop, they will cut your arrows to length for you. Do not attempt to saw it off to yourself because fiberglass arrows tend to be finicky when cut. In some cases, there are arrows pre-cut that you can purchase, typically in a small bin instead of in a box; but they are only meant to be used for practice. Do not attempt to compete with them or hunt with them.

Tip 47: Shoot the same arrows every time.

Over the years, you will develop quite a collection of arrows such as arrows that you bought, arrows that you found, and arrows that you played with. Your quiver may end up looking like a rainbow of fletching's, but you must use the same type of arrow every single time. Different arrow spines and lengths fly differently. You may test different types of arrows through the years, and eventually, you will settle on your favorite set. When you find that set, stay with it, especially when you are practicing or competing. Switching between different arrows mid-heat will result in inconsistent shot patterns. One set may stray left while the other strays right. It will confuse you when you are on target for one shot but way left for another. Consistency is key in archery, same form, same bow, same arrow, every single time. As you dial in, you will find yourself closer and closer to zero, as long as you remain consistent in your delivery.

Tip 48: Use a proper quiver.

The quiver is one of the most iconic parts of archery gear. In movies and TV shows, the back quicker is portrayed as a backpack that stores your arrows, but unfortunately, it is not as practical as some may think. Not only does a quiver on your back makes it difficult to retrieve your arrows, but it can also interfere with the motion of your draw. There are only two practical types of quivers, the quiver belt, and the bow quiver. The quiver that hangs from your belt is the most convenient and easiest way to store your arrows. It removes any fumbling and fidgeting for an arrow, as well as stays out of your way. It is the typical quiver that most archers use for practice and competition. The other type of quiver attaches to your bow. Typically for hunters, the bow quiver makes it easier to move around in the forest without getting caught up in any branches or bushes. These quivers hold much fewer arrows but compact everything you need for archery into your bow. I would suggest a belt quiver in most cases because it holds the most arrows and is the most convenient for retrieving your arrows. It may not be as flashy as a quiver on your back but trust me. It will save you a lot of hassle in the long run.

A popular quiver amongst hunters, this bow quiver attaches directly to your bow, reducing the amount of equipment that a hunter must carry.

Tip 49: Tune your bow.

Bows are not unlike rifles. They have to be tuned on occasion to ensure that everything is aligned. Things like making sure the arrow rest is leveled to making sure that the sight is lined up are all things that periodically need to be checked upon. In terms of aligning your bow, it can mostly be done by eyeing the straightness of your string and the alignment it has with your sights. There are several things that can affect this, the tightness of your bolts, your cam, etc. Generally, this can be fixed with some loosening and tightening of specific components. Your local bow shop can fix up your bow in a matter of a few minutes for free. The sighting in of your bow can be slightly more difficult, but it only requires an Allen wrench and a target. Remember that everything is the opposite when adjusting sights. Moving the sight down will make you shoot high, and moving it up will make you shoot low.

Tip 50: Do Not Dry fire your bow.

The last thing to know when building your own bow is that you must never dry fire it. Dry firing is shooting the bow with no arrows. This is the ultimate taboo and will surely break your bow. Compound bows are the biggest victims when dry-fired. Parts fracture and splinter due to the enormous pressure applied to the limbs. While dry firing is common practice with firearms, the only way to practice with a bow is to actually shoot the bow. Aside from your bow shattering, it could also lead to serious injury. The nature of the bow is to apply a great amount of force to an arrow. That force is what helps the arrow fly great distances, but when you take away that arrow, the force has nowhere to go but back into the bow. This is what creates the shattering and splinting, especially in a fiberglass arrow. I unfortunately dry fired by accident once, and luckily it was just my strings that suffered. I recall not even reaching my anchor point before the string slipped from my fingers. Even at a half draw, it was enough to force to derail the string of my bow. This is also why a release can be helpful to prevent any accidental misfires.

Chapter Review

The great thing about being an archer is that you can completely customize your bow. It would not be easy to find two bows belonging to two different archers that are the same. There is a sense of pride in that, and when you build your bow, you must keep this in mind. What about your bow is going to make it unique to you and you alone. Will it be the draw weight, the arrows you use, or perhaps the attachments you choose. The term "everyone is different" has never been more accurate for archers. Your bow is built to your needs and is built to your liking. It is a once-in-a-decade build, and you must devote your time and money to it. An average archer is not likely to replace their bow for many years, so it is no understatement to say that you can never over-invest in your tools when it comes time to do so.

Lesson 6: Preserving the Longevity of Your Investment

The 10 Essentials to Make Sure You and Four Bow Remain Unharmed.

Tip 51: Invest in a good case.

An outrageously expensive case is not necessarily needed, but I would not suggest getting just any case for your bow. Especially for competition bows, being able to preserve your bow during the transportation is very important. At the minimum, I would suggest a hard case instead of a soft case for your bow. It will prevent anything within the case from breaking or move due to any form of impact. The last thing you would want is your sights to move because you accidentally bumped it against a table on your way to the competition. Even in the case of hunting, you will not have the opportunity to adjust your sights right before a hunt. This is why a hard case is suggested over a soft case. Outside of transportation, a hard case is better for storage for your bow as well. Technically, a compound can be hung in a workshop by its cam, and it will be fine. A workshop, however, is not always available to everyone. A bow has to be stored in a closet or garage for those with a more compact living arrangement. When anything is stored for long periods, many things can happen to it. Rodents can get into your storage, or things may shift and collapse. Either case can seriously damage your property. That is why a hard case is suggested. It can deter rodents from chewing at your strings and protect your bow from any heavy objects that might accidentally land on it.

Tip 52: Store your bow during the off season.

Just like any sport, there are seasons to archery. You will find a couple of months of the year that you don't touch your bow. The off-season for hunters is 80 percent of the year. Competition archers typically have an event somewhere at least once a month, but even professionals will take a break every now and again. During this downtime, it is important to stow your bow properly. Do not leave it in your shed for long periods and expect it to be able to shoot like no time has passed. It is important to keep your bow stored in a dry, climate-controlled area. Avoid basements and garages because the cold and flood hazards could result in the warping of the bow (especially traditional bows). Compound bows are tougher to break, but that does not mean you can stuff it in a basement and completely forget about it. If you have space, hanging your bow on a bow rack is the best way to prevent any warping. If the space is not available to you, a good bow case in a dry climate-controlled area will do just as well.

Tip 53: Take apart your traditional bows.

Traditional bows may have the least parts involved, but they require some extra attention in terms of maintenance. Long-term storage is not like compound bows where you can hang it up or put it in a case and leave it. While compound bows rely on the cam system to launch arrows, traditional bows rely on the tension of the limbs. If you store your strung-up traditional bow for a long period of time, it may result in the weakening of the limbs or even damage. Simply unstring your bow to release the tension on the limbs when you store it. Keep in mind during the hunting season, or a short period of time where you are shooting fairly frequently. It may be alright to leave your bowstring. Leaving your bowstrung overnight will not break the limbs, but it may warp if not stored in a climate-controlled environment. I left my traditional bow strung up in the garage for a summer, and when winter came, its limbs were very warped. This can be very dangerous with traditional bows. Weakened limbs can shatter when you try to fire them, possibly resulting in serious injury. If you notice any cracking or splintering in the limbs of your traditional bow, take it to a shop right away. You may need to replace it.

Tip 54: Get lots of arrows.

If an archer ever tells you that they have never lost an arrow, they are lying. Especially in the beginning, you will lose a couple of arrows every time you go to the range. You may try to test yourself and shoot at a further distance and end up completely missing the target. 3D targets, in particular, will be the bane of your existence in the beginning. Due to their smaller and awkward size, you will most likely overshoot or undershoot the target a few times. Even the most professional archers will lose an arrow now and again. Keep a healthy supply of arrows stocked for these occasions. Arrows can be fragile when mishandled or when fired at dense objects. It is not uncommon for the fletchings to be ripped off occasionally or for the shafts to splinter. I am not suggesting that you buy a huge bulk of arrows in one sitting. That would be foolish and expensive. I would suggest stockpiling your arrows over time. It would be naive to think that you can manage with the same six arrows for the entirety of your archery career.

Tip 55: Don't cheap out on broadheads

Disclaimer, broadheads are only meant for hunting. Do not use a broadhead for practice, and vice versa. If you do go hunting, a proper broadhead is essential for swift and humane kills. A broadhead is designed to cut through anything in its path. A practice tip is not. If you were to use a practice tip for hunting, it would cause a lot of pain for the animal and not kill it. The design of a practice tip is to pierce, not cut. It is essential to know the difference. Piercing the target will cause minimal damage. It may pass entirely through, but it won't be enough damage actually to finish the job. A broadhead is meant to cut, so it causes massive damage and hemorrhaging during

the arrow's trajectory because understanding this trajectory will help you adjust your aim for different ranges. It can also be helpful for hunters shooting in tight areas with a lot of possible obstructions. All things are affected by gravity. It's no different than throwing a ball. The farther you intend to throw it, the higher you have to throw the ball. This especially comes into play when adjusting your sights for further targets. Traditional bows, in particular, have to change their aim to shoot further away due to it being much weaker than a compound bow. Archers who shoot without sights have an intimate relationship with their bow and should have an understanding of its capabilities with an arrow.

Tip 59: Remove any unnecessary equipment.

The arrow is a finely balanced tool with deadly capabilities. In its raw form, any skilled archer can put it to good use. It would be detrimental to the purpose of the bow if it had an excessive amount of equipment attached to it. Do not try to trick out your bow like it's some sort of race car. Stick to the necessities, and it will serve you just fine. By unnecessary equipment I mean, wearing a quiver during practice or a large bow stand when you are hunting. I have witnessed some attempt to attach a knife to their bow or a laser pointer to the edge of their stabilizer, all cool in theory but very unnecessary. Outside of the necessary equipment, less is more.

Tip 60: Dress the part

Depending on your intentions with archery, whether for hunting or competitions, you have to dress the part. It may be okay to shoot in flip flops and sweatpants during practice, but it will not bode well in a competition or hunting. Understand that there is an unspoken dress code amongst archers, and shooting/hunting in streetwear will not help you achieve your goals. In terms of practicing, remove any jewelry that could get caught in the bowstrings. A long necklace may infringe on your shooting and possibly hurt you, and a nose ring may get caught when you draw the string back to its anchor point. Not only could these accessories hurt you, but they can also possibly damage your bow. When shooting in any situation, it is best to keep your body clear of anything excessive.

Chapter Review

Archery is an expensive sport. Unlike most traditional sports, you can't "play" at your local park. The equipment itself cost upward of five hundred dollars easily. This is not to mention the cost of joining an archery club or the cost of maintenance and replacement of your equipment. It makes sense that you would want to preserve the longevity of your equipment, whether it's doing several micro-purchases to prevent a larger one or investing in quality equipment that will last you much longer. Things like investing in a good case, using string wax, or even simply taking apart your bow when you are not using it will add years to its life. If well maintained, a bow can last an archer a lifetime. You might never have to replace your bow if you treat it right, and while you might have to do some minor maintenance here and there, you will never need to buy a new bow unwillingly.

Lesson 7: Developing a Sound Body and Mind

The 10 Essentials to Being Physically and Mentally Prepared to Dive into the World of Archery.

Tip 61: The Faster the Arrow, the Better

Speed is an essential factor in archery. The faster the arrow, the more deadly it is and the more accurate it is. The arrow's speed is determined by several things: wind resistance, arrow weight, and draw length. Although, the most significant factor in the arrow's speed is the draw weight of the bow. A forty-pound draw weight will not launch the arrow as fast as a bow with 100-pound draw weight. That is why in hunting, the higher draw weights are favored, while in competition, it is given a maximum; so that there are no unfair advantages given to the stronger archers. Of course, none of these matters if you are only strong enough to use a 40-pound bow. Ultimately, weaker archers are at a slight disadvantage. They have to shoot a little more accurately and have to adjust a little more at longer distances. If you intend to hunt or go to competitions, you should develop your body to shoot with higher draw weight bows.

Tip 62: Get stronger

The bottom line is that archers have to be strong.
Strong enough to pull 60 pounds or more. For
traditional bow archers, not only do you have to pull
60 pounds, but you have to be able to hold it.
Shooting often and consistently will naturally develop
your muscles to the point that the draw weight
becomes easy for you. However, that does not mean
you can't help quickening the process by weight
training on the side. If you research bows with hefty
draw weights, you will find that all the men reviewing
the bows are fairly big. That is because outside of
archery, they also go to the gym. The more powerful
the bow, the more powerful the archer has to be.
Becoming stronger will not only make pulling the
string back easier, but it will also make practicing less
strenuous on your body. The less stress you have on
your body, the more you can practice and the faster
you can develop your skills as an archer.

Tip 63: Work out your shoulder.

Three major muscle groups are engaged when
shooting a bow. One of them is your shoulders. Your
shoulder (deltoids and trapezius) are the muscles that
pull back the sting of your bow. When shooting for
extended periods, this muscle group is likely to be the
first to feel the fatigue of shooting. The more you fire,
the more difficult it will seem to pull back the weight
of the string. To counter this fatigue, you can lower
your draw weight, or you can get stronger. While
reducing the draw weight may seem the most

convenient, it sacrifices the benefits of high draw weight. To strengthen your shoulders, I suggest these workouts three days a week. Keep in mind that you should gradually increase in weight over time.

The overhead shoulder press:

This workout can be done standing or sitting. For higher weights, you will most likely have to sit. Take a barbell or a dumbbell in each hand and simply raise it above your head. You want to be sitting/standing straight. Keep your hands and arms at a 90-degree angle parallel to the floor and raise the weights up and back down slowly. You must have complete control of the weights that you are lifting. Do not be ashamed to start at a lightweight. Attempting to lift heavier than you can handle will result in injury.

Front and Lateral raises:

This is a difficult lift for even the biggest bodybuilders, so stay at a lighter weight. Take a dumbbell in each hand, and let it hang at your sides. Raise it in front of you with arms fully extended, then alternate lifting the weights to your sides (your body should be in the form of a T). When bringing the weights back down, let it fall to the front of you at your belt buckle rather than to your pockets. This minor adjustment will prevent your shoulders from rubbing against the cartilage in your socket.

Bent over row:

This workout is the most similar to pulling back the string of your bow. You will need a bench for this workout. With the weight on the ground, you want to orientate your body parallel with the ground, one knee and hand on the bench, with the opposite leg on the ground and the other hand lifting the weight. Pull the weight up to your ribs, and hold. Similar to pulling back the string of your bow. It is important not to twist your body when pulling the weight. Doing so makes the lift ineffective as well as dangerous. A big jerk and twist can seriously hurt your back.

Do these three workouts regularly, with progressively heavier weights, and your shoulders will strengthen with time.

Tip 64: Work out your back.

Your back muscles engage when you reach the anchor point in your draw. Essentially, your back determines how long you can hold your anchor point. This is more important for traditional bow archers. Compound bow archers don't feel the full weight of the draw, thanks to the cam system. Regardless, developing a strong back will make it more comfortable for you to aim for long periods. Being able to engage your back fully is essential to proper form and follow through. The most effective back exercises open up your chest. There is a wide variety of exercises that can strengthen your back, but here are three to begin with.

Resistance band pull apart:

This can be done anywhere and requires only one piece of equipment. Grab a resistance band with your hands shoulder-width apart and stretch the band. Squeeze your shoulder blades together and hold. This can be a good warm-up exercise or just a stretch that you do throughout the day. Not only will this improve your strength, but this can help with your everyday posture as well.

Lat pulldown:

Perhaps the most common and widely popular back exercise is the lat pulldowns. This exercise engages the biggest muscles in your back, your latissimus dorsi. It is a staple piece of gym equipment in nearly every main brand gym facility. Choose a weight you can handle and pull the bar down to your chest, squeezing your back. Do a weight that you can handle, and remember to do this slowly and in a controlled manner.

Seated Row:

The seated row is another staple part of most main gyms. Very similar to the bent-over row, but rather than one arm at a time, you will be pulling weight with both. Sit on the machine and lock your legs out. Grab hold of the bar, and make sure to sit straight up. It would be best if you weren't hunched over when you are doing this lift. Pull the cable to your chest and squeeze your back. This exercise will engage multiple muscles in your back. Be sure to hold it for a second before you bring the weight back out.

Do these three exercises three times a week, and gradually increase your reps and sets. Unlike chest exercises, there is no such thing as too many back exercises.

Tip 65: Work on your grip

Without a release, pulling the string back will be difficult, especially for new archers who learned to pull back with three fingers. To mitigate this situation, develop your grip strength. One of the most unfortunate and embarrassing things an archer can do is misfire the arrow mid-draw. If this happens to you often, your grip strength is too weak, or the bows draw weight is too high for you. Perhaps, both. To improve your grip strength, try these simple exercises.

Farmer walks:

Farmer walks are simple, take some heavyweights in each hand and walk a great distance with them. If you have a gym membership, use two plates of significant weight and take a lap around the gym's perimeter. It may seem like an easy exercise, but the stress it puts on your forearms will fatigue your entire body with time.

Tennis ball squeeze:

The most straightforward way to improve your grip is to grip things. Everyone has seen those grip genies. It has been a part of every household at some point or another. This same function can be achieved with a tennis ball or racketball. Any palm-sized ball that can provide enough resistance for your hand to squeeze will improve your grip. However, don't try and squeeze a baseball. You want to have a little give with the ball.

Standing cable w/ towel:

This exercise can be a standalone or incorporated into previous exercises such as seated rows or lat pull down. If you were to use a towel as your bar instead of a traditional bar at the gym, then you would be forced to grip a lot harder than normal. You could also use a towel for the cable machine and do triceps extension if you wanted to. This is essentially what a standing cable w/ towel exercise is. It is primarily a triceps workout but incorporates a lot of grip strength.

Do these exercises twice a week with gradually increasing weight, and your grip strength will slowly improve. If you intend to shoot without a release, then you will need to do these exercises more frequently, at a higher weight.

Tip 66: Be flexible

When I say be flexible, I don't mean the splits. When I say flexible, I mean with your back. Archery requires proper posture, and for your form to be at its best, you need to have good back posture. If you stand with your back to a wall and hands up like you are forming a W, you should be able to touch both elbows to the wall simultaneously. If you cannot, then you have an issue. Stretch your upper back regularly and be mindful of your posture. Often yoga can help with flexibility or something as simple as morning stretches. When firing your bow, you must follow through with your release. What I mean by this is that when you release your arrow, you pull straight back, but sometimes when an archer is not flexible enough, they tend to jerk left or right instead. This will throw the arrow off trajectory. That is why posture is so essential. The archer needs to be able to remain still and straight like the path of their arrow.

Tip 67: Be comfortable holding at your anchor.

It is no secret that patience is key to good aim. You should not and cannot rush a good shot. That is why you should get comfortable holding your bow at its anchor. Now that you have gained the strength to do so, get comfortable holding the anchor. Take your time, breathe, and aim. This may be exceptionally hard for traditional bow archers, but it is a skill that needs to be prioritized. In competition and hunting, accuracy is critical, and it will not be achieved by launching an arrow in a general direction. To practice this, hold the anchor a second or two longer than you usually would. Take a breath and live in the moment. If you are struggling to maintain the hold, then the weight may be too much for you.

Tip 68: Watch videos of yourself

Do not be embarrassed to watch videos of yourself. It is an excellent technique to ensure that you are using good form. The best lessons come from a place of humility, and you may find that you were doing something wrong when you thought you were doing something right. Watch multiple repetitions of yourself over time and see the progress that you make. The minor adjustments will show eventually. A timelapse may help reveal some glaring flaws that you may not see in hours of footage.

Tip 69: Be patient

Understand that this will take time. You will not get stronger after one exercise or be more flexible after a couple of stretches. You won't be able to increase your bow's poundage after just one week. Gaining the strength and knowledge to improve as an archer is not like video games. It is not instant gratification; you are in for the long haul. The sooner you accept that the sooner you can begin the journey one arrow at a time. This applies to your patience with the development of your skills for your craft. In hunting, you will sit in a tree for hours, and in competitions, you need to take your time with each shot. I have said it once before, and I will say it again. Never rush your shot.

Tip 70: Do not be ashamed to take classes.

Lastly, the most helpful thing anyone can do is take classes. Both physical training classes and archery classes would be beneficial to the readers of this book. There is no shame in taking classes. They are full of useful information that you can take with you into the future. Taking classes helps you develop a fundamental understanding of skills, such as archery courtesies, safety tips, rules, and fundamentals. If you link up with a physical trainer, you will learn about lifting weights, good stretches, diet tips, and critical exercises to stay healthy. Overall taking classes is never a bad idea. Research your nearest archery club for details about beginner to intermediate classes and local events.

Chapter Review

Archery is far more physically taxing than most realize, and it requires a significant amount of training to be good at the sport. It would be best to have a strong body and a sound mind to shoot many arrows in one day. Typically, a bow has a draw weight of fifty pounds, and if you want to shoot more than a dozen arrows during practice, you will have to get used to pulling that weight. Not only will you be lifting that weight upward of a hundred times during training if you have a traditional bow, but you will also have to hold that weight while you aim. New archers find themselves fatiguing very quickly at first because they are not used to the bow's weight. Of course, due to the nature of the sport, the higher the draw weight, the better. This leaves archers no choice but to get stronger. Exercises like overhead shoulder press or Lat pulldown can strengthen the essential muscles you need to draw back and aim your bow. With time your body will adapt to the needs of the sport, and shooting a hundred arrows will seem effortless.

Lesson 8: Accuracy is the Name of the Game

The Ten Essentials to Good Accuracy

Tip 71: Know the rules of archery competitions.

Archery is the sport of marksmen, and accuracy is prioritized over everything. If you have any interest in competitions, it is essential to have pinpoint accuracy. The rules of each competition change slightly depending on several factors. It is essential to know the rules of the sport that you play. If you do not, then you are not playing that sport. Archery is no exception. Unrefined and uncontrolled archery is barely target practice. Know what you are doing and what is expected of an archer.

The following are the traditional bow rules of the USA archery competition.

Gender: Male and Female

Age Class: No separate categories. All shoot as "Senior."

Five equipment divisions will be made:

A. *Traditional longbow (TLB):* Wood longbows/flatbows and similarly made from natural materials without arrow rests or shelves.

B. *Modern longbow (MLB):* wood longbows containing modern man-made materials. Arrow rests, or shelves are permitted.

C. *Traditional recurve (TR):* recurve or similar bows with wood risers.

D. *Traditional Asiatic bow (TAB):* European, Asiatic, Turkic, Mongolian or similar, made from natural materials.

E. *Modern Asiatic bow (MAB):* European, Asiatic, Turkic, Mongolian or similar, made with modern materials.

General Rules:

A. A longbow is defined as a bow with bowstring contact only at the string nocks.

B. Stabilizers or counterweights or bows built up to serve the same function will not be allowed except for short stabilizers in the recurve division (see below.)

C. Protruding bow sights (except for traditional recurve) will not be allowed. However, for longbows, a movable band/"o-ring" or rubber band on the bow limbs will be permitted if this band is no larger than 1/8th inch wide or high. An alternative allowed reference method is the moveable "Point-of-Aim." This cannot exceed a height of 6" if on the ground or be larger than 3" in diameter.

D. No cushion plungers or similar mechanical or metal apparatus shall be used. However, for the side of the bow where the arrow meets, it may be built out slightly with a leather pad.

E. Arrows will be fletched with feathers. Points shall be of a type that will not inflict undue damage to target faces or buttresses. Point weight may be of any value. All longbow and Asiatic bow competitors must shoot wood arrows. Recurve shooters may shoot wood or aluminum. The maximum arrow diameter is 9.3mm.

F. Finger protection in the form of finger stalls or tips, gloves, shooting tab, or tape (plaster) is allowed to draw, hold back and release the string, provided it does not incorporate any device to help in holding, drawing, and releasing the string. For example - mechanical releases or hooks are not permitted. A separator between the fingers to prevent pinching the arrow may be used. On the bow hand, a glove, mitten, or similar item, may be worn.

G. Binoculars and spotting scopes are not permitted.

The World Archery Rule book is much more extensive and cannot be covered within the context of this book. I strongly encourage anyone serious about competing to read and understand what is expected of you for each competition you intend to compete in.

Tip 72: Know the rules of hunting.

The rules of hunting change depending on what country you are in and what state you are hunting in. For example, you may be allowed to use an AR with a magazine in one state but only allowed a bolt action rifle in another. Bows are less customizable when it comes to performance, so there may not be as many rules for hunting with a bow, but that does not mean it is without limits. The typical minimum draw weight for a bow in the US (United States) varies between 30-40 pounds. In addition to this, some states do not permit the use of electronic devices to be attached to your bow. The only exception for this rule is flashlights and rangefinders.

If a hunter does not comply with the state hunting laws and a game warden where to catch them, the repercussions could be costly. Unfortunately, the bow is not as powerful as a gun, and as archers and hunters, we must accept that. The hunting laws are in place to protect the wildlife from mistreatment and inappropriate ways of elimination. I strongly encourage any that are considering hunting to read up on the rules in place for bow hunting season and study and understand their prey.

Tip 73: Watch videos

In today's modern age, a lot of people learn from videos on the internet. It would be foolish to consider yourself above the help of the internet when learning archery for the first time. There are a plethora of knowledgeable archers sharing what they know through videos. There is no shame in taking tips from a YouTube video. However, I urge people to do extensive research on the topic of study before watching the videos. Incorporating the mechanical understandings of the bow with the visual examples depicted in the videos will help you study and learn more efficiently. When you watch a video for specific tips, be sure to listen to what they are teaching. It is no different from taking a class. You either listen and take in all of their knowledge or skim through the video and take away nothing.

Tip 74: Wear your glasses!

I am guilty of this. I suppose it is harder to forget your glasses for those who have a stronger prescription strength, but we tend to forget our glasses on occasion for those like me who have a milder prescription. Depending on how strong your prescription is, your vision may be impaired when aiming at the farther targets. This is a frustrating reality of having a bad vision. You mustn't forget your glasses at home when leaving for the range or a hunt. Clarity is a crucial factor to accuracy, and accuracy is the most fundamental factor in archery. It would also be beneficial to invest in contacts if you shoot often. Glasses are essential because they help you see the details of the target, but they can be a bit of a nuisance when you are trying to look through the sights of your bow. Contacts may be the best option when it comes to comfortability and clarity. Regardless, if you wear glasses or contacts, you must wear them to shoot. It is highly frustrating to shoot blind. It feels like you are not shooting at your full potential, and that is because you are not. Come to each practice, tournament, and hunt at 100 percent, or you will be kicking yourself in the butt all day.

Tip 75: Focus on groupings!

When practicing, it is easy to fall into the mindset that getting a bullseye is everything. I mean, why not? It is dead center, a sign of perfect aim. Unfortunately, accuracy is not so black and white. A proper showing of accuracy is a tight grouping. A tight grouping shows that you are aiming in the same spot every single time. It is a sign that you have great control of your bow, and being off-target is at the fault of your sights, not you. Say you were to land a bullseye for one shot, but you have two or three in the outside circle of your targets. That means you are not shooting at the same spot every time. Your arms are swaying and shooting at different points. You may be jerking one-shot or flinching on another. It creates inconsistencies with your form to make you either a great archer or a bad one between shots. Being able to remain completely still while you aim is difficult, so when shooting for accuracy, trying to replicate the same thing every time is more realistic. For example, when aiming, your bow will inevitably sway to some degree. If you harness the swaying to move in a pattern of your choosing and release at the same point every single time, you will have effectively replicated the same shot over and over. This is your rhythm. Find the rhythm of your breath and the sway of your bow. Once you have mastered that rhythm, shooting will feel more natural, and your accuracy will improve. Remember, the tighter the grouping, the better.

The term "To Robin Hood an arrow" means to split one arrow with another. Essentially to stack shots so precisely that they land in the same hole, this should always be your goal when shooting.

Tip 76: Do not adjust your aim.

An archer's common mistake when sighting their bow and testing their accuracy is adjusting their aim mid-heat. If your arrows consistently land to the left, but you keep adjusting your shot, your groupings will be all over the place. Aim at the center every single time and create a tight grouping. With the information you gather from your groupings in relation to the center of the target, you can adjust your sights. This will not work if you aim center for one shot, then adjust and shoot high left on the next one. If you adjust your aim after one shot, you might find that it is still off on the next. Adjusting your aim is something you do after being completely certain that your sights are at fault. No archer is perfect, and even the experts will mess up a shot on occasion. Do not panic and aim true. When you have eliminated your sights as a factor for your off-target shots, it may be your human error causing the missed shots, which is okay. With practice and time, accuracy will come easy to you.

Tip 77: Mark your shots

A helpful tool for adjusting your sights is marking your shots. After a long day at the range, your target will be covered in holes. It will be challenging to determine which shots were old and which ones were new. This can be troublesome when you are trying to dial in your sights. You may mistake an old grouping for a new grouping. Marking your shots is a simple way to remedy this predicament. Bring markers to the range and mark your shots. Your target will look like a paint pallet, but you should see a pattern in the groupings if your groupings are tight. These patterns will help you inch your shots closer and closer to your intended target. This same method is used for tournaments and rifle shooting.

Tip 78: Use aiming drills.

Aiming drills are effective ways to build your muscle memory. If you struggle with consistency, then it's crucial to create a routine and use aiming drills to teach your body to aim the same way every single time. Here are a couple of aiming drills that will help with your consistency.

Blind Shooting:

Blind shooting is not blind shooting. It is shooting with no intent to aim. This may sound weird, considering we are talking about accuracy, but this drill is meant to familiarize your body with the motion of shooting a bow. Stand at a close distance and focus on the feel of the bow. Memorize your anchor point and how it feels to draw the arrow-straight back. When you get a good grasp of your shooting motion, you will know when something feels off. You will recognize if your draw was too short or if your sights are not aligning with your eyes. The feel of the bow is half the battle.

Shoot fast:

This may go against everything I have been preaching, but some archers suffer from perfection. What I mean by this is that they try too hard to get their aim perfect. It is overthinking a sport that developed from instincts. The greatest archers in ancient history did not have the same technology as us. They did not have sights, or a rest. They had their instincts, and even in today's modern archery, the core of an archer is their instincts. Shooting at a faster tempo does not allow you to aim for too long. It removes the overthinking that nervous archers tend to do and forces them to shoot primarily with their instincts with minimum aiming.

Resistance bands:

Tie a resistance band to your foot, then another one to your aiming arm. You do not need a super high resistance, just enough to push you out of your comfort zone. Shooting with resistance bands will make it more difficult to control and aim your bow but will train your body for the added weight. Once your body has grown accustomed to the bands, you can take them off, and you will find that everything feels much lighter. The control and weight of the bow will feel relatively easy compared to shooting with the bands, theoretically making it easier to aim.

These three drills are good tools to incorporate into your practice whenever you can as a warmup drill before your training or competition.

Tip 79: Do not be afraid and be confident!

Any form of marksmanship can be somewhat scary, but it is essential to understand that a bow is just a tool that is entirely under your control. It cannot hurt you unless it is being misused. This is not to say that archery is without some risks. Freak accidents can occur that will result in some injuries. Rather than focus on not being afraid, I want you to focus on being confident. Confidence is vital in any sport. When you shoot your bow, I want you to feel empowered and in control. I would even go as far as to say that you should be cocky. If you are shooting at 20 yards but are confident that you could shoot at 70, then the target will appear much closer to you. A baseball player is always confident they can hit a home run, and a soccer player is always confident they can score a goal. Expecting greatness out of yourself sets you up for success. Expecting any less will result in a weaker performance. It is a matter of mentality and believing in your capabilities.

Tip 80: Relax your grip.

Tension is the enemy of accuracy, and gripping your bow too hard is the leading cause of misplaced shots. When shooting your bow, you must be as relaxed as possible. You do not want to stiffen up to the point that your body is shaking from strain. Not only is that exhausting, but also detrimental to your accuracy. A simple way to alleviate this problem is to relax your grip. When shooting, you want to be gripping your bow at all. The handshake method is the most straightforward example. When you draw your bow back, your gripping hand should be extended out like it is going for a handshake. The draw weight of your bow will pull the bow back into your palms so it will not drop. This creates a tension-free point of contact with your bow, removing the unnecessary factors caused by too tight of a grip. It will allow you to focus on your aim and releases solely.

Chapter Review

Accuracy is prioritized over everything in a marksmanship sport, but the definition of accuracy can be blurred at times. For example, what's more accurate? The 1/3 bullseye with the other two missing scattered far-left and far-right, or the three arrows that are all far-left but grouped tightly? The answer would be the one with the tighter grouping. The tighter grouping is a sign that you have excellent accuracy because you aim in the same spot every time. You can do several things to improve this, such as aiming drills, relaxing your grip, or even simply wearing your glasses. Although ultimately it comes down to confidence, aim at the same spot every time, knowing that you will hit it and you will. Keep this in mind while you mark your shots and focus on groupings. As you adjust your sights, you will walk your way into a bullseye, but you must be patient and not adjust your aim between shots.

Lesson 9: Being a Veteran Archer

The 10 Essentials That Every Veteran Knows.

Tip 81: Stretch your strings.

A veteran archer will replace their bowstrings once a year for a target bow or every two years for a hunting bow. When it comes time to replace the strings for your bow, it is essential to remember that strings do stretch after a certain amount of use, and brand-new strings will make shooting your bow feel different. Essentially, there is a breaking-in period for your new strings. Some archers enjoy the feeling of brand-new strings, while others find them off-putting and stiff. Regardless, the strings will stretch with each arrow fired from it, and you will begin to synchronize with the new feeling. It is no different from getting a new pair of shoes. You must walk a couple of miles in them to mold them to the shape of your feet. You must shoot a few dozen arrows to stretch the strings to your bow. This is a process that every archer must go through because continuing to shoot with worn-out strings may result in mechanical failure, or overly stretched strings may decrease your overall draw weight. If you don't shoot too often, then you may not have to replace your strings as often, but I assure you they will need to be replaced at some point.

Tip 82: Use a rest with the least resistance.

Arrow rests can be pretty complex the more expensive they get. The simplest arrow rest is known as a whisker biscuit, and while it may be a classic, it tends to slow the arrow down. If you want a rest that allows the arrow to travel at its maximum speed, then you will need a drop-away rest. This arrow rest drops out of the arrow's way when launched. This provides the least resistance to the arrow's flight path compared to the whisker biscuit that an arrow must fly through. Regardless of the arrow rest you settle on, the arrow's speed is the key factor to think about. I tell you to get a rest with the least resistance because resistance from the friction that the rest creates can significantly slow down the arrow. Any type of rest already decreases the resistance an arrow would receive if it were on the arrow shelf (no rest). Admittedly this may be one of your more expensive investments. The good news is that you can't go wrong with whatever you choose.

Tip 83: Hold your follow-through.

Holding your follow-through is more of a veteran tip for beginners. Holding your follow-through is a helpful crutch to keeping proper form. A problem with most beginners is that they tend to shift their bodies or flinch during releases, resulting in misplaced shots. Holding your follow-through forces you to stay on target until the arrow has left your bow. That small mental note that you will hold your form until after you've heard the arrow hit its target will counter any flinching or last-minute shifting when you release. If you do flinch or shift during your shot, it will reflect in your form. Look down your sights and confirm you are still aiming where you wanted to. Some shifting is inevitable, but if you are way off your mark, then you will know. It is an excellent self-critiquing technique when you do not have a spotter or trainer to correct you.

Tip 84: Get good at guessing.

Sometimes archery can be a guessing game, especially when hunting and shooting at odd ranges. If you do not have a range finder, you must learn and understand what certain ranges look like. When you have been shooting for a while, your depth perception will develop to understand the distance of targets. If you are familiar with a football field, then you will have a better understanding of depth. This can be helpful when shooting at your range as well. At a traditional archery range, targets will be marked with the distance they are at. On your own, you won't have such luxuries. This skill does not only apply to your depth perception but in the adjustment of your shots. Traditional bows don't typically have as many attachments as a compound bow and need a little more adjusting when shooting off target. The slang "Kentucky windage" comes to mind when addressing this tip. Kentucky windage is when a shooter corrects their aim to account for wind. To put it simply, If the wind is pushing your shots left, aim right. Being able to shoot with precision despite an imprecise situation makes or breaks the best archers.

Tip 85: Number your arrows

Numbering your arrows helps you sort out your shots when shooting a large volume, especially when practicing for an event. Repetition is key to practice, and shooting many arrows in one heat at the range will maximize your time. The problem with shooting many arrows is that you lose track of the order you shoot in. It's essential to keep track of this to see the pattern and progression of your shots. Perhaps there is one specific shot that you remember messing up. Numbered arrows will help you distinguish which shot that was. When it comes to sighting your bow or refining your form, it's crucial to know the results of your adjustments. It can be difficult when over a dozen arrows are scattered on the page, and numbering the arrows will help you sort the shots in that heat out. This is especially helpful when you are trying different things between shots. For whatever reason it may be, shooting different arrows or bows between shots, adjusting your sights, trying to tweak your form. All of this can result in different results when shooting, and the farther you shoot from, the harder it will be to see where the arrows land. Keep this in mind when you are finding your form.

Tip 86: Don't practice on moving targets.

In Hollywood, archers are always perceived as these expert sharpshooters that can shoot anything, moving or stagnant. Unfortunately, these great and magnificent acts of archery are far from realistic. Even hunters do not shoot at moving targets. They wait for the opportune moment where the animal is staying still with their broadside presented. Archery is a sport of patience, and shooting at moving targets is more of a party trick than a practical skill. I find that many people who take on archery at first find it difficult to distinguish fantasy from reality. Make no mistake that there are archers out there that are fully capable of shooting moving targets, but the practicality of the skill will never be put to the test. In competitions, you will shoot at a stationary target, and in hunting, shooting at a moving target will surely only waste your arrows and scare the prey. This is not to say that you cannot shoot at moving targets. If you wish to take on that challenge, nobody is stopping you. It will require a great deal of mental strength and repetition to master that craft, but you must understand it will not help you with competitions or hunting.

Tip 87: Keep an account of the wind.

I've discussed Kentucky windage to some extent, but the term usually only applies to firearms. The wind has much more of an effect with arrows than it does with bullets. The fletching of arrows catches more wind than a small bullet and thus results in much more shifting mid-flight. Keeping an account of the wind will help you land your first shot without walking your shots in. This can be a useful skill, especially with outdoor competitions. Wasting a shot to test the strength of the wind will waste your points. Some competitions will tell you the direction and strength of the wind. With enough time and effort, you can predict how far an arrow will stray depending on the wind speed and direction. This is a much more difficult skill but an essential one when shooting at competitions. Correcting your shot trajectory before the first shot can result in either good or bad results. Mastering reading the wind will improve your chances when trying trajectory correction.

Tip 88: Zone out

Being in the zone is a commonly used term for individuals that are deeply immersed in their craft. Things that typically require a significant amount of skill become easy. Being in the zone is total immersion. You find a level of focus unprecedented to your typical state of mind. It's difficult to force yourself to be in the zone because your natural flow is unconsciously coming to the surface. The wonderful thing about being in the zone is that you forget about everything else, except the task presented before you. Your complete undivided attention is what makes being in the zone so effective, and with enough time committed to the sport, you will be able to go in the zone much more often. Until such experience is under your belt, try your best to zone out in the moment. This is a kind of partial immersion. What do I mean by this? It means not to overthink the situation and just shoot. Overthinking hurts more than it helps, and your nerves will most likely get the better of you. When shooting, it is best to enjoy the day and shoot with no expectations. Like the blind shooting drill, zoning out is shooting without the pressure to shoot accurately. With time and experience, accuracy will come after. Some may be nervous around spectators, or perhaps they hold a tremendous amount of burden by placing many expectations on themselves. It is reasonable to have these fears, but you must forget about everything outside of archery to perform at your best.

Tip 89: The bow drop

A sign of good technique is when a bow drops out of the archer's hand after a shot. In an earlier tip, I mentioned that you should loosen your grip, but veteran archers will take it further and not hold their bow at all. Gripping the handle of a bow will make your arm too tense and ruin your aim. You will see this quite often in traditional bow competitions. The archers drop their bow after a shot because they are not gripping the bow tightly at all. Tension is the enemy to accuracy, so when you shoot, you want as much of your body to be as relaxed as possible. The only tension in a perfect shot is the tension of the limbs applying force to the arrow. Any tension with the grip or holding your breath does not apply force forward to the arrow's momentum but rather left, right, up, and down affecting the accuracy of the shot. The bow drop may seem uncomfortable initially, but it is a good sign that you are inching towards the perfect shot.

Tip 90: Understand that it may take years.

It takes 10,000 hours (about one year and two months) to master a skill that roughly translates to 4 hours of practice, five days a week for nine years. Unless you are a sponsored professional, nobody has that kind of time to commit. We all have lives outside of archery, and realistically the most committed archers only practice a couple of hours a week. Unless you started at an early age, this would take years to master. You may feel proficient with time, but you will have to compete and practice for many years to become a grandmaster archer. It is best not to overthink about the hierarchy of archery but rather let time take its course and with it your skills. These 101 tips will be helpful in the short term, but only time will help you overall. Commit some time every week to practice. If you can't practice, then play with your bow, anything to get your hands-on experience. I like to take apart and put together my traditional bow. I believe that understanding the ins and outs of your bow will make you a better archer overall.

Chapter Review

There are several signs of a veteran archer. Just like any other skill, people learn by trial and error. Archers are no different and, over time, have developed several taboos or tips that have helped them throughout their careers. When you go to an archery club, watch the older archers and observe their habits, such as numbering their arrows or dropping their bow at release. These are both signs that they have been shooting for a while. Years of practice have taught them to shoot without gripping the bow and simple tips and tricks to make their life easier. Rituals develop with time, and you will find yours soon enough. After years of practice, you will develop little tricks that will improve your overall performance, and you, too, will be considered a veteran archer.

Lesson 10: Weird but Helpful Tips

The 10 Weird Essentials to Your Overall Improvement

Tip 91: Cover up!

By cover up, I do not mean to wear a sweater because of decency. By cover up, I mean you should wear an arm guard. An arm guard is especially needed for those new to archery because, more than likely, your form won't be that good in the beginning. Due to improper form or hand placement, the bowstring can hit your arm during the release. With time, your form will improve, but you may find that your arm is in the path of the bowstring on occasion in the earlier stages of development. Being slapped by the bowstring, especially with high poundage bows, can be very painful. Your arm will indeed develop quite a bruise if the string contacts your skin. Most bows will come standard with an arm guard. It can help soften the impact on your skin if the bow meets your arm. Some archers wear it for peace of mind, while others with high draw weights wear it because of their compromised form. I find wearing a thin long sleeve sweater or a hoodie to be just as effective. Essentially, clothes that can provide you with an extra layer of protection without getting in your way. An arm guard is a cheap but useful piece of equipment that could save you some pain. I suggest getting one decent arm guard and sticking with it until you no longer need it. The bowstring can hurt, but it will never do enough damage to your arm guard to the point of needing it replaced.

Tip 92: Try the Mongolian draw.

The Mongolian draw is very rarely used in today's archery. Essentially, it has the archer pinch and pull back the string with just the thumb rather than the three fingers on the string method. This draw is mainly used in Asian archery but developed during the rule of Genghis Khan. The Mongolian empire relied heavily on horseback, so they had to create smaller bows and faster reload methods. The ability to shoot from horseback has given the Mongolian empire the reputation of being some of the best archers in history. Understandably, some modern-day archers model their form after these revered archers of the Mongolian empire. To say one draw method is better than the other is subjective. Whatever feels more natural is what's best for the archer, whether the Mongolian draw or the traditional draw. Regardless of if you are trying to find your draw or playing around with new techniques, the Mongolian draw wouldn't be a bad place to begin. Adapting and learning new techniques is part of being a good archer.

Tip 93: No acrobatics

I began archery when I was incredibly young and watched Lord of The Rings. I wanted to be just like Legolas. I was just a kid and only played with my bow on occasion. As I grew up a little, I became fond of superheroes like the Green Arrow or Hawkeye. Since I was older and slightly more athletic, I began to pretend I was just like my idols. I would tumble and try to shoot the bow. I would slide and shoot, ride my skateboard, and shoot. I did everything I could in my parents' basement. I thought I was the next Robin Hood, but when I finally upgraded to an adult bow, I found that my skills did not transfer very well. The 15-pound draw of my kid's bow gave me the illusion that I could shoot fast and effortlessly. You can imagine my disappointment when I could barely pull back my new 50-pound compound bow. Not to mention I went from shooting 15 yards max to shooting 20 yards minimum. When I took my first class, I got grilled for my awful form and lousy aim. I'm not telling you this to embarrass myself, but to tell you the reality of archery. We are not superheroes, and we'll never have to shoot on that impossible level. You get good by grounding yourself to the basics. The crazy acrobatic stunts of a kid with a starter bow can get someone seriously injured. After all, archery is a deadly sport.

Tip 94: Watch the fingers!

It doesn't occur often, but there are incidents where the archers' fingers are in the arrow's flight path and get badly skewed. In most scenarios, your fingers would be entirely out of the way of the arrow. Often the arrow is too long to get behind your fingers at full draw in the first place. Some archers prefer shorter arrows. Even Olympic archers seem to risk their fingers with shorter arrows. Of course, they dedicate their lives to the sport and aren't likely to make such mistakes. Even so, it's a gruesome injury that can happen to anyone who is not careful. To prevent this from happening, focus on your grip on the bow. It should be loose and outstretched for a handshake. The bow should be sitting in the meaty part of your palm with your fingers tilted out and downwards. On most occasions, you wouldn't need to worry about your fingers but knowing is half the battle. Simply being aware will be enough to prevent an accident.

Tip 95: Learn the history

This tip is not so much to improve your ability, but rather a strong suggestion. The coolest part of archery is its history, and you would be missing out if you chose to ignore it. It is one of the oldest and most reliable tools in human history. From Africa to Europe. Longbows, Mongolian bows, recurves, and compounds. Archery has changed with time, and it has supplied a vast history to the sport. Learning the history of archery might ignite a passion for the sport that was absent before. The history of archery teaches you a lot about shooting that would be considered unorthodox now. Like the Mongolian draw, a lot of skills and tricks of archery have been lost in time. Some archery historians have brought back old techniques and are pioneering a new wave of archery. A simple google search or a short video on YouTube can teach you a lot about a sport with a lot of history to discover.

Tip 96: Shave

It may seem strange that facial hair has anything to do with archery. Robin Hood has such a magnificent mustache, after all. Plenty of archers have facial hair, so why does it matter? Well, it doesn't, unless you have an enormous thick beard. When you bring the string back to your anchor point, it should sit up against your face, typically either by your cheek or your chin. Usually, the hair on your beard wouldn't be in the flight path of the string, but if your beard is thick and curly enough, it can be. I'm not sure of a much more uncomfortable way to shave, but like everything in this strange chapter, this is a rare occurrence. Shaved or not, it is best to keep things out of the flight path of your string.

Tip 97: Develop a ritual

There is a comfort in routines and traditions. At this point, you should have developed a shooting routine that you follow to ensure good form, but doing a pre-game ritual can set the tone for your entire shooting session. The 2016 Olympic gold medalist pulled his bowstring three times before every match, and Lebron James throws chalk in the air before basketball games. Rituals like these can help you get in the right mentality to perform at your best. It's like horoscopes, they may not have any physical effect on your performance, but it does influence your psyche which in turn does affect your performance overall. It's a sport of analytical thinking, and mindset is half the event.

Tip 98: Wear a chest guard.

Archers wear chest guards for various reasons, most commonly to keep their chest and clothing out of the way. You will see chest guards worn by all the Olympic athletes because of how close they hold the string to their body. A chest guard, much like an arm guard, is meant to protect an archer from harm. You will see them most paired with traditional bow archers because of the form they are taught. Traditional bows tend to be a little more unpredictable than compound bows, and as such, are more challenging to aim. To compensate for this, archers get as close to their bow as possible to align their eyesight with their arrow. Women might find a chest guard to be more helpful and more necessary than men.

Tip 99: Listen to the arrow

When you shoot long enough, you will begin to distinguish the different sounds an arrow makes. Some of these sounds can tell you a little about the quality of your shots. If the arrow whistles in the air it means, it's traveling at high speed. Depending on your arrow, arrow rest, and draw weight, your fps can increase or decrease. The thudding of an arrow on targets can tell you if your arrows are flying in straight or at an angle. If they are hitting the target crooked, you may need a different arrow spine for the draw weight of your bow, or the alignment of your bow might be off. Hunters might find the most use out of the tip. The sound an arrow makes when hitting prey is very distinct. A loud thud vs. a quieter one may indicate that you hit a shoulder bone. This can be very problematic depending on your draw weight and broadhead; a Sholder bone shot might not be able to penetrate all the way through. The look and listen method come to mind. Observing your performance does not have to be solely done through watching videos of yourself.

Tip 100: Make a team!

It may be hard to believe, but archery is a team sport. In the Olympics, the sport is divided between individual and team events. While all the archers are equally skilled in their craft, the team event seems to be the more popular of the two. In a team event, two teams of three will compete in a shot for shot shoot-off. Each archer per team is allowed one shot per heat in a best of 4 ends. Of course, we may not all have such lofty ambitions, but the camaraderie of a team sport affects us all the same. It's nice to be on a team, it makes practice more fun, and it forces you to hold yourself to a higher standard. If you mess up in an individual event, you only disappoint yourself, but in a team event, others rely on you. This added pressure can help elevate your performance and breakthrough that plateau that you may or may not have hit. Team sports have a way of bringing out the best in all of us, and I challenge all archers to put themselves in a situation that holds them accountable for their performance.

Chapter Review

There are many things any archer can do to improve. Minuscule adjustments that may seem like they won't help but do. Weird things like shaving or adjusting your draw form can help. If you believe in superstitions, these minor adjustments might be what you need to get yourself over a mental hurdle. Most of all, develop a team! I cannot emphasize enough how practical shooting on a team can be. It is the last thing new archers think about when picking up the sport, but it is perhaps the most effective tip in this entire book. As you continue to improve, don't be afraid to try some different tips because it may be the thing that takes you out of the plateau that you've hit.

Lesson 11: One Last Thing

The Most Important Tip in This Entire Book!

Tip 101: LOVE THE SPORT!

If you are not enjoying what you are doing, what is the purpose of doing it? Learn to appreciate and love archery. Archery may seem like a serious sport with high stakes at times, but we all started as kids who wanted to be Robin Hood. It's okay to shoot on occasion and not take it too seriously. Yes, being a good archer is a lot of work. No, it does not have to be your life. If you love to shoot and enjoy the feeling of firing a few arrows downrange, that's all you need. You don't need to be the next Olympic gold medalist; you can be just another person trying out a new hobby.

I fear that the sport of archery has been painted in a bad light. From a distance, it may seem like a club too prestigious to get into. Although, upon a closer look, you will find it is filled with fun and humble souls. Train regularly, and you will naturally progress in the sport. Forcing yourself to improve on command will not work, nearly as well as just having fun and letting it happen naturally. If you genuinely love a sport, you will excel in that sport despite any physical or economic challenges that you face.

About the Expert

Miguel Rocha began archery when he was 12 years old. In the beginning, it was about mimicking his favorite superheroes, but as he grew older, the sport became second nature. Competing in local events with Olympic aspirations, Rocha honed his skills to become a master of the sport. Now in his late 20's, archery has become more of a hobby than a career. Even so, he practices regularly to retain the skills he developed growing up. He is a writer, father, and always and forever an archer.

HowExpert publishes quick 'how to' guides for all topics from A to Z by everyday experts. Visit HowExpert.com to learn more.

Recommended Resources

- HowExpert.com – Quick 'How To' Guides on All Topics from A to Z by Everyday Experts.
- HowExpert.com/free – Free HowExpert Email Newsletter.
- HowExpert.com/books – HowExpert Books
- HowExpert.com/courses – HowExpert Courses
- HowExpert.com/clothing – HowExpert Clothing
- HowExpert.com/membership – HowExpert Membership Site
- HowExpert.com/affiliates – HowExpert Affiliate Program
- HowExpert.com/jobs – HowExpert Jobs
- HowExpert.com/writers – Write About Your #1 Passion/Knowledge/Expertise & Become a HowExpert Author.
- HowExpert.com/resources – Additional HowExpert Recommended Resources
- YouTube.com/HowExpert – Subscribe to HowExpert YouTube.
- Instagram.com/HowExpert – Follow HowExpert on Instagram.
- Facebook.com/HowExpert – Follow HowExpert on Facebook.

Printed in Great Britain
by Amazon